Heart
&
soul

Stefka Harp

Heart and soul
© Stefka Mladenova 2014, revised 2015

All rights reserved. No part of this publication may be reproduced, stored in a retrieval system, or transmitted in any form or by any means, electronic, mechanical, photocopying, recording or otherwise, without the prior written permission of the author.

National Library of Australia Cataloguing-in-Publication entry

Author: Harp, Stefka, author.

Title: Heart & soul/Stefka Harp.

ISBN: 978-0-9923040-0-3 (paperback).

Subjects: Australian poetry — 21st century.

Dewey number: A821.4

Published with the assistance of www.wordwrightediting.com.au

Images courtesy of clker.com.

www.stefkaharp.com

… Contents

Acknowledgements v
Dedication vi
Introduction vii
God bless 1
The Oracle 2
Victory 3
Love and live 4
In God we trust 6
In faith we walk 8
The walk of life 10
God loves you 11
Live in spirit 12
Procrastination 13
Everlasting peace 14
Heart and soul 16
Soul mates 17
Silent voice 18
God within 19
My 10 commandments 20
Inner beauty 22
Respect others 23
Rejoice 24

Destiny 25

Unique 26

Faith 27

Reincarnation 28

Forgivenes 29

Divinely humble 30

Ocean of love 31

Trust the Divine 32

God is as you know it 34

Joyful day 36

Eternity 37

Respect is love 38

Soul searching 39

Life is a challenge 40

Focus on the positive 42

As you think, you are 44

Divine compassion 46

Trust is earned 47

Sending out bad energies 48

Protection from bad energies 50

My writing style 52

Divine temple 53

About the author 54

Acknowledgements

I wish to express my deep and sincere gratitude to my parents for teaching me the value of life — how to love and be happy as well as show kindness; and to my siblings, for being a part of my life.

My thanks, too, to the Australian Government for opening the door for me to migrate and become a permanent resident; to experience a different kind of life, culture and customs, which has been very enriching, enlightening and eye-opening. I am very grateful for the opportunity I have been given and guided to get to the point I am at.

Sincere gratitude to:

- my daughter for her patience and loving assistance in proofreading my work
- Alison Leader for her editing
- my publishing advisor for assistance given
- my niece Maria and my loyal friends who were willing to read my manuscripts and give constructive comments and feedback.

Dedication

Everything I write and have written so far is dedicated to my family and the divine within, which has guided me through life. At times my ignorance and oblivion to the facts revealed has led to strife and suffering. But these experiences have given me the much-needed fuel for my writings, and I hope they will help others. Life is like a jigsaw puzzle. Some things are meant to happen so that the pieces fit within that puzzle.

S.H.

Introduction

It is a well-known fact that thoughts are energies — what we think, we bring.

Many times you become aware of your feelings, and somehow you think of a person for no reason at all. This person is possibly thinking of you and sending thought messages relating to you. Perhaps they are thinking what a wonderful person you are, what a beautiful soul you have — and similar thoughts. You feel elated and happy without knowing why.

Embrace the feelings. Endorse them with love and return to the sender, whoever he or she might be, giving them exactly what they're sending you. You get what you give, so they say.

On the other hand, if the feelings are adverse, it means this person is thinking of you in a negative way, whether in hate, jealousy, envy or fear. There is a possibility they are cursing you and wishing evil things upon you.

Whatever you do, don't retaliate. All you have to say or think is: I send your thought energies back to you, whoever you are, endorsed with my sincere and pure love; and leave it at that. Immediately you will feel calm and light as a feather. A burden has been taken off your shoulders.

Those energies are not yours and you can't deal with them. They have to go back to their rightful owner. If this is not done, then more negative energies around

Stefka Harp

you will build up and start to drag you down. You might blame different causes for your mishap.

If by any chance you release negative and undesirable thoughts, try and catch them in the moment and cancel them. That is all you have to do to nullify the energy, and they won't go anywhere or be in existence. If you realise what has happened after some time has passed, ask for forgiveness in thought, whether you talk to the universe, God or the Divine within. It works every time. Get into the habit of doing it every evening. Forgive and ask for forgiveness, sending the energies back and cancelling your wrongdoings.

The poems you're about to read are structured in a way that you can read and chant them.

The more they're repeated, the more thought energy is released and the more strength accumulated. These are chants and prayers for health, happiness, love, forgiveness, peace and harmony.

It's all here for you to discover the power of your mind and the universal connection and thought energies.

Stefka Harp

Disclaimer: The author is expressing beliefs and views based on her life experience. There is no intention to offend anyone who has contrary views. The poems are fun to read and in the process can bring a positive and loving attitude.

Heart & soul

Good, kind and caring you are,
Opulent in every aspect,
Destined to do all that is good.

Blessed you are to give
Love and kindness to
Everyone that comes by, that is why
Serenity and peace
Shall be yours eternally.

Stefka Harp

The Oracle says,
Heavens above bring you luck,
Earthly life, peace and serenity.

Ocean of love,
Rivers of happiness
And countless blessings
Come your way.
Live and rejoice
Eternally, the Oracle says.

Vast and ever-changing life is,
Impulsive and impelling,
Celebrate the challenge, for
The kind soul you are.
On and on, marching by
Regardless of setbacks,
Young and vibrant journey through life.

Love the creator, marvel the creation,
Open your heart, verbalise the need,
Valse to the tune and pray for good health,
Everlasting prosperity and success.

Address others with love and respect,
Nurture yourself and care for others,
Delight in their good health and success.

Live the day as though it's your last.
Innermost wisdom reigns supreme,
Vast freedom, infinite peace and serenity,
Eternal intelligence is leading the way.

In good times and bad,
No one but God is always there.

Goodness me! It is so true,
Only you would know and feel
Day in, day out.

When doubt and fear knocks on
Ever so strong, heavens above!

Trust in God and do not give in.
Remember, faith is nearby,
Unobtrusively but unmistakably,
Spring up and meet faith,
There will be no fear.

Stefka Harp

It is like so,
No matter what,

Fear not, faith is near,
Accept it with all your heart
Into your life, feel
The power of the prayer,
Heavenly so, will get you there.

When worries and uncertainty set in
Eroding your faith,

Worn out and exhausted, take
Action and declare a war, by
Letting faith and trust in God
Kindly show you the way.

Through gloom and darkness
Heavenly so, into the light
Eternally forever so.

Wake up in the morning
Accelerated and energised,
Life is too short, so waste it not,
Keep moving, doing your best.

Oh God and your mighty love
Forever and ever and ever.

Love is God and God is light.
Insofar as you do it right,
Follow your heart and for
Evermore, whatever you do, do it with love.

Heart & soul

God is pouring his love
Over our hearts and minds,
Demanding nothing in return.

Love yourselves, respect others, he says.
Only love illuminates the way,
Very faithfully leading so that
Everything we do is done with love.
Second best is not good enough, he says.

Yes, I repeat it dear soul,
Obey the wisdom within,
Understand the union with the one.

Leap for joy, you have a life,
Inside you there is a spirit, oh so kind,
Vital as the divine child,
Embrace it for happiness to find.

It is like so, you will be greeting
None other but the spirit within, that

Shapes and helps us sail through.
Precious life is, so waste it not.
Invoke positive thoughts,
Rejoice living in the now
Immensely so! Yesterday has gone,
Tomorrow never comes, it is always today.

Press on with loving thoughts,
Reclaim the inner peace,
Organise your affairs,
Challenge the feelings, and
Receive Blessings from the Divine.
Attune to the silent voice, the
Silent voice within
That gives strength and
Innermost trust.
Necessary to make a decision,
Allow failure if you must,
The procrastination will dissipate.
Inevitably, you will be
Onward marching by,
New ventures to try.

Stefka Harp

Everything I do, I do it with love,
Vale of years, river of tears and
Everything turns out just right.
Ray of hope fills me with might,
Life I cherish day and night,
Always and forever with God my light,
Sincere and sweet I shine bright,
Treasure the divine by my side,
Insofar I have done right.
Now and always blessed I am, oh
God, you are the core of my life.

Peace-loving and passionate I am,
Embracing life over again,
Another enjoyable day
Captivating the essence of the soul,
Endless happiness and joy.

Heavens above bring you luck,
Everlasting happiness and love.
Accept the Divine within,
Rejoice in the inner beauty
Time after time, tremendously so.

Adore the goodness in your heart,
Nurture the soul, nourish the body,
Divine power will do the rest.

Send loving thoughts
Out to the world,
Utmost sincerity and forever more,
Let love and divine light embrace your life.

Sure as you can be,
Oneness of two souls is not rare,
Undeniable as is life,
Let the Divine within be a guide.

Majestically as it should be,
Angels appear to be fleeting,
Temples of God, always and forever,
Extraordinarily compatible souls
Sweet as the nectar of the gods.

Seek the Divine without a question,
Instil love and patience,
Let God within guide
Eternally so, justly and sincerely,
Now and forever, insofar as the
Truth will come out.

Verbalise your prayers with meaning,
Obey the wisdom within,
In God's time, not ours,
Certainly the silent voice you will hear,
Embrace it, it is ever so dear.

Grace and honour upon all,
Only way to go,
Dare to be fair and yearn to know.

Wade in, weary traveller,
Infinite God is always there,
Tenderly dear and close by,
Hence, waiting for you to ask, and
If ready to know and do not fear,
None other but the silent voice you will hear.

My 10 commandments

I trust in God, the heavenly Lord.

I have faith the Lord will provide.

I send love to God, myself and others.

I am kind and caring.

I do it gracefully, expecting nothing in return.

I am humble, God is working through me.

I hope for the best and do no less.

I use words to pray, praise and encourage.

I send blessings to the world.

I feel peace and serenity reign supreme.

Inevitable as can be,
Noble and glorious,
None other but the Divine,
Ever so more,
Resides within.

Brilliant shining light, I
Embrace and nurture,
Allow it to flourish
Unrestricted and of free will.
Tender thoughts and words, will instil
Years of graceful beauty and eternal youth.

Respect for others is a step forward,
Enjoy being respectful as a reward,
Seemingly attracts the same,
Persist and you will gain
Everlasting peace without fail. The
Choice is yours, meet and greet
The life you desire and live well.

Or if ignorant, there will be feelings of pain,
Take courage and proclaim,
Hence happiness is here,
Ever so near and dear.
Resist adverse thoughts by showing respect,
Sheer joy within you could detect.

Rejoicing I am
Every moment of my life.
Joyful it is, to say the least,
Only because I make it so, to have
Innermost peace and serenity.
Chanting and praying for
Everlasting happiness, prosperity and success.

Heart & soul

Devotion to the Divine and yourself,
Expressing well wishes to all
Saintly so, requesting the best,
Then remember to say thanks.
Indeed, praise as well as blessings
Notably will get you there.
You certainly will get what's given out.

Utmost understanding,
No one is better, only unique,
Indefinite and forever.
Question not, doubt not,
Uplift the Divine within,
Emerge from the shadows of the deep.

Fear not, faith is here,
An angel told me so.
I believed it and planted the seed.
The seed has grown
Heavenly big to take me through life.

Realisation of the possibility that
Everyone lives another life
If certainly you choose to.
Numerous memories of past lives
Conceived and carried over,
Always and forever more.
Ripping out what had been sown.
No one is ever overlooked in getting
Another opportunity to right the wrong.
The ultimate outcome is to learn
In quest of love and happiness,
Obstacles to be removed with grace,
Now and forever, loving thoughts in their place.

Forgive indefinitely,
Only forgiveness will set you free.
Rejoice in letting go,
Gracefully so.
Imagine nothing but the best, the
Very best for yourself and the rest, give
Endless blessings to the world.
Never stop loving yourself.
Embrace and accept for who you are
Seize the moment and enjoy
Serenity will follow for sure.

Develop a loving attitude,
Integrate patience and calmness,
View the world in a positive manner,
Inspire happiness and choose to be happy.
Nurture and pay attention to your thoughts,
Embrace them, and change the unwanted ones.
Last but not least,
Yell 'I love myself'.

Honour and respect always,
Unconditionally to yourself and your neighbour.
Merriment is sure to follow,
Beaming with love, hope and joy.
Live long and show love to others,
Endurance will reach the goal.

Occasion to be celebrated,
Centuries of changing and perfecting,
Either in or out,
Always on the go,
Never still even for a moment.

Onward marching by
First and foremost.

Legendary to say the least,
Open and in tune,
Vast and mighty grand,
Emerging from the core of yourself.

Terrific way to start the day,
Radiant as sunshine in every way.
Utmost trust in the Divine,
Sanctuary for the soul to thrive,
The ultimate outcome is being alive.

Tranquility throughout day and night,
Hard and fast will come upon you with delight,
Entirely submerging body and soul in light.

Heart & soul

Dance to the tune within,
Incredible way to be living,
Vigorously and fast.
Instil love, grace and trust.
Nobly show gratitude galore,
Earnest well-wishing to bestow.

Generous and always kind,
Only on your mind,
Divine love to find.

Infinitely, it's a must,
Smile and let it last.

Always and forever more,
Serenity you are to know.

Youthful body eternally,
Our divine right certainly,
Utmost peace and tranquility.

Kindle the desire of innocence to manifest,
Nurture the idea deep within and caress,
Openly vow not to run aground
While progressing in leaps and bounds.

Impression of all of the above on your mind,
Transformation and divine elation you'll find.

Journey every moment of life anew,
Once in a while, celebrate too.
Y not?
From one moment to the next, is the
Ultimate reality, whatever the test,
Learning to live in the present is the best.

Dazzle as you journey through life,
Attuned to the Divine,
Yes, it is up to you to shine.

Heart & soul

Endless and vast,
Tremendous transformations,
Evolving and perfecting,
Renewing and rejoicing.
Near and dear,
Insofar as marching by,
Trust in God and your inner self,
Yearn for fairness and everlasting peace.

Rejoice and shine,
Even just for being alive.
Small step a big leap no doubt,
Peace loving child is all about.
Empower yourself with positive thoughts,
Come along and take note ...
Time for spiritual growth.

Impress respect on your mind
Straight away, and be kind.

Love for yourself and the world to cheer,
Over and above, whatever you do, be sincere,
Vigorously at your best,
Enabling respect and love to manifest.

Sheer joy is to find your inner self,
Obey the inner wisdom and dwell in
Unity with the Divine,
Letting pure love guide.

Sincerity with yourself is a must,
Eliminating the doubt fast,
Attuned to the silent voice,
Reassurance is a good choice,
Captivating the essence of the higher,
Harmoniously and gracefully to transpire.
Instantly loving thoughts to inspire,
Notably becomes loving word with time,
Gently nourishing the soul and
               soothing the mind.

Larger than life are the challenges, I agree.
Inspiring my inner-most strength, I decree.
Fair enough to take note and endear,
Encouraging myself to go on and persevere.

Important it is to acquire patience and be kind,
Simplify what matters most with a smile,

Approaching issues one at a time.

Heart & soul

Clarity of challenges makes fear disappear,
Humble and sincere I cheer,
Awareness comes to the fore so clear,
Loyalty to myself is dear.
Love makes life worth living, I
Enjoy the challenge and whatever dealing.
Nothing comes closer to push myself forward.
Gracefully I face them all, marching by,
Excellent way to get on with life.

Failing to become aware of your thoughts is
Opening the door for events to befall,
Created by the very thoughts sent out,
Unleashing good or bad, no doubt,
Sure enough would be coming around.

Obvious it is, the energy is coming back,
Nevertheless you can change all that.

Think only what you desire,
Hence this is what will transpire,
Expect a positive attitude to acquire.

Heart & soul

Persevere with your pursuit and be aware,
Only loving thoughts, instead of despair, are
Sufficient to get you there.
Impress it on your mind with loving prayer,
Tranquility felt enough to cheer,
Indeed positive attitude to revere,
Vigorously saturating mind and heart,
Enchanting the soul with delight.

As amazing as it sounds,
Success or failure come around.

Yesterday's thoughts created today's destiny,
Omen for you to know,
Up and away – faith to restore.

Thoughts are powerful energies, make sure
Harmonious and loving thoughts you have galore.
Indeed, keep going and persevere,
Necessary to become aware is quite clear,
Karma in action can be severe.

Yearn to give love and be kind,
Out you go and light you find,
Unlock the secret of the Divine.

Accelerate your desirable thoughts,
Receive what you've asked for, it's
Exactly how divine power works.

Diverge from the crowd
Into being yourself, it is all about
Valid argument without doubt.
Indeed, the statements you make,
Neither more nor less, are what you create
Ever so, make no mistake.

Consider being praiseworthy.
Others will respond likewise,
Magnifying the well-wishing energy,
Perfect environment for emerging
An angel within with compassion.
Small step, you're not wrong, but
Soul divine is going strong.
In no time a ray of hope will shine
Over you and the world to guide,
Now and forever to be one with the sublime.

Heart & soul

The trust everyone longs for earnestly,
Remarkably, doesn't always come fast.
Undeniably trust is earned by actions; it's a
Sign to shift gears and do recollection, that
Those actions we display need detection.

Indefinite and no second thoughts,
Situation to review those sent-out words.

Errors to be removed and written off fast,
Action speaks louder, like a blast.
Reason for us to be true at once,
Never to turn away is a must,
Evidently, we need to express trust,
Deviation of it would turn everything to dust.

Safeguard your thoughts
Ever so they become words.
Next, they are powerful energies
Destined to reach the target.
In no time, and no sound of a trumpet,
Nevertheless, they always come back
Guaranteed, those energies, to bellow

Overnight, to roost and crow
Under your roof for sure.
Thoughts sent out stronger ten times more.

Bad feelings feel wrapped around
Announcing it is payback time.
Deal with it on the count of nine.

Heart & soul

Express forgiveness without delay,
Nasty energies nullified every day.
Embrace love instead and bless,
Regret the wrong doing without stress.
Gratitude shown for becoming aware,
Inevitably, with a loving prayer, to
Elevate the soul and prepare
Soul divine to flair.

Stefka Harp

Prime focus is to be aware at least that
Released thoughts are energies,
Onward always in search of
The intended target, aiming to reach.
Eventually when they do,
Catastrophic events could be in it for you.
Terrible feelings would follow too.
Invisible might seem, so you dismiss
Overall the suffering will persist
Non-stop until you exist, unless

Fairly soon you recognise and know the
Reason for those feelings and more.
Out you send them back
Mentally, and do not regret.

Breath of love makes it clear
Always! And perseveres
Diligently without any fears.

Excellent way to deal is to forgive,
Nasty energies gone back, better believe.
Embrace love and send to the sender,
Repeat it as often as you can.
Gloominess around will dissipate
Innate calm will manifest.
Evidence of bad energies long-gone
Straight back where they belong.

Magical moment to say the least,
Yes, when I write about the beast. I

Write what comes to mind,
Revise it any time,
Insofar as I am doing well,
Talent I would like to dwell,
Initiating words of grace,
New ways for me to praise,
Generously without dismay.

Selecting any quiet corner
Today and any day to ponder
Yes! I lay the first word on the line,
Later I make it rhyme,
Ever so, to reflect the crime.

Heart & soul

Dedication is in need,
Immediate attention to proceed.
Vanquish the temptation of greed,
Invoke healthy habits instead.
Notice the process of your thinking
Essential to know what you are feeling.

The body is the temple,
Extraordinary divine sample.
Meanwhile it is time to be an example.
Purity and holiness to seek
Laugh all the way and greet
Earnest spirit in elevation indeed.

About the author

Stefka was born during World War II in a small village tucked away in the foothills of a big mountain in Eastern Macedonia.

Her family, like others in the village, gained their food from the land. It was a self-sufficient household. This lifestyle built much confidence in her and her siblings.

She migrated to Australia in 1972, where she still resides. She finished her degree, and a diploma in counselling, and gained jobs in the welfare sector.

The last seven years before retirement were spent in the DV sector. While working with people she noticed the power of thought in relation to destiny. She believes that when people change their thinking and implement positive and loving thoughts, life changes for better. Prayer, forgiveness, hope and faith go hand in hand with a positive attitude.

Academic achievements

Diploma of Community Services Management

    Southbank Institute of TAFE 2006

Diploma in Counselling

    Australian Institute of Counsellors 1993–1994

Bachelor of Arts Degree (Major Psychology)

    University of Queensland 1989

Economics, book keeping & accounting

    Business Studies College (Macedonia)

www.ingramcontent.com/pod-product-compliance
Lightning Source LLC
Chambersburg PA
CBHW061250040426
42444CB00010B/2332